ST 5/16

Nature's Children

BEAVERS

Elin Kelsey

 Grolier

FACTS IN BRIEF

Classification of North American beaver
    Class: *Mammalia* (mammals)
    Order: *Rodentia* (rodents)
    Family: *Castoridae* (beaver family)
    Genus: *Castor*
    Species: *Castor canadensis*

World distribution.   North American species exclusive to North America; related species *(Castor fiber)* found in Europe and Asia.

Habitat.   Rivers, streams, lakes in wooded country.

Distinctive physical characteristics.   Flat, wide scaly tail; webbed back paws; large orange-colored front teeth.

Habits.   Builds dams and lodges; lives in family group called *colony*; mates for life.

Diet.   Bark, twigs, leaves, roots, water plants.

Published originally as
"Getting to Know . . . Nature's Children."

This series is approved and recommended by the Federation of Ontario Naturalists.

Canadian Cataloguing in Publication Data

Kelsey, Elin.
  Beavers

(Getting to know—nature's children)
Includes index.
ISBN 0-7172-1894-5

1. Beavers—Juvenile literature. I. Title
II. Series.

QL737.R632K45 1984   j599.32′32   C84-099386-2

Sold and distributed in the United States by Grolier Educational Corporation.

Contents

Beavers: Who and Where ..... Page 7

Beavers Up Close ..... Page 8

Seeing, Smelling and Hearing ..... Page 12

Champions in the Water ..... Page 14

Clumsy on Land ..... Page 17

Special Teeth for Special Food ..... Page 17

Special Food ..... Page 18

The Beaver At Work ..... Page 22

Getting it Home ..... Page 24

Building the Dam ..... Page 27

Nature's Engineers ..... Page 28

Beaver Meadows ..... Page 31

A Home of Sticks and Mud ..... Page 32

Making it Comfortable ..... Page 35

The Beaver Family ..... Page 38

Beaver Babies ..... Page 43

A Lot to Learn ..... Page 44

Growing Up ..... Page 44

Words to Know ..... Page 47

Index ..... Page 48

When you think of beavers, the first thing that probably comes to mind is the expression "busy as a beaver." People have been thinking of beavers as eager, hard workers for a long time. For example, there is an Indian legend that tells of the Great Spirit building the earth with the help of beavers. This would certainly have been a big enough job to keep a lot of beavers very busy. And it would have been a good job for them because they are excellent builders.

Now let's find out what makes beavers such good builders and what is keeping them so busy today.

Beavers: Who and Where

There are some beavers in Europe and Asia, but most of them live in Canada and the United States.

The beaver has no close relatives, but it does have some distant cousins. You can recognize them by their teeth. All beavers have big, very sharp front teeth that they use for cutting. Squirrels, rats, and gophers have sharp front cutting teeth too. Scientists call animals that have special teeth like these rodents. The name comes from a word that means "to gnaw or chew"—which is just what all rodents love to do!

Where beavers are found in North America.

Beavers Up Close

The sturdy beaver is the largest rodent in North America. You would have to be quite strong to lift an adult beaver. In fact, if an average-sized eight-year-old and a beaver were sitting on either end of a teeter-totter, their weights would about balance.

An Amazing Tail

There is no mistaking a beaver's wide, scaly tail. It looks like a pine cone that has been flattened by a steam-roller! This amazing tail serves many purposes. When the beaver is swimming, it steers itself through the water by shifting its tail from side to side. If it is towing a heavy log, it moves its tail to balance the weight. A frightened beaver slaps its tail against the water with a loud *thwack*! The sound tells other beavers to dive for safety.

A Beautiful Coat

The beaver's coat may not be as remarkable as its tail, but it is much more beautiful. It is soft and silky, and can range from golden brown

to rich, dark brown in color. It is also very warm—which is probably more important from the beaver's point of view!

Why is the beaver's coat so warm? Because it has two layers. The outer layer is made up of long shiny "guard" hairs. Underneath, is a thick, woolly layer of shorter fur. It is a coat worth taking good care of, and beavers do just that. They even have a built-in comb for the purpose—two double claws on each hind foot. These claws can open and close, rather like a pair of tiny pliers, and the beaver uses them to untangle its fur and to comb out any twigs or clumps of dirt.

As well, all beaver have a pair of glands near their tails where a special oil is made. They spread this oil through their fur with their paws. Even after an hour of swimming, a beaver's body stays dry and cozy inside its oily, waterproofed coat.

In the wintertime keeping warm and dry is especially important to the beaver. This beaver is grooming its fur to get ready for the swim home.

Beaver paw prints.

This waterproofing is important because beavers spend much of their time cutting and peeling branches underwater. Most animals would soon get waterlogged if they tried this, but beavers never do. They have furry lips that close behind their front teeth to keep the water out, so they can work just as well underwater as they can on land.

Very near the glands where oil is made is another set of glands, called castors, where castoreum is made. Castoreum is a strong-smelling oily substance with which beavers mark their ponds and lodges to let other beavers know who lives there.

Seeing, Smelling and Hearing

Beavers have very small ears and eyes. But their hearing is excellent, and they see quite well—at least in daylight. They find seeing in the dark just as hard as you do, however. Yet beavers do most of their work at night. Instead of relying on their eyesight, they use their sharp senses of smell and hearing to direct them and alert them to danger.

Front paw.

Back paw.

Champions in the Water

With a flat tail for steering and strong, webbed back feet to supply the power, beavers are perfect water travellers. Their bodies are streamlined for swimming. Holding its tiny fists tight against its chest, a beaver glides through the water with only its head above the surface.

Beavers are also terrific underwater swimmers. Their large lungs can store lots of air, and most beavers can hold their breath for about ten minutes.

No matter what kind of fancy flips and dives a beaver makes, it is never bothered by water getting into its nose or ears. Beavers have special muscles that seal their nostrils and ears when they are diving.

A beaver's eyes are protected too. Thanks to an extra pair of see-through eyelids that close over its eyes, a beaver can see just as well underwater as it can above.

Clumsy on Land

Getting around on land is another story. Imagine playing tag in the woods with swim fins on your feet. You would trip all over your big, floppy feet and be easy to catch. Beavers have the same problem. With webbed back feet the size of ping-pong paddles, beavers are very slow and awkward on land.

For beavers, water means safety. When they do have to go ashore to cut trees, they listen and sniff the air carefully to make sure no one is coming.

The more a beaver uses its teeth, the sharper they become.

Special Teeth for Special Food

A beaver's front teeth are very special. Like your fingernails, these large teeth never stop growing. A beaver must chew to trim its teeth just as you must clip your nails to keep them from getting too long.

The outer surface of these front teeth has an incredibly strong orange coating. As the beaver chews through pieces of wood, the backs of the teeth wear down faster than the strong orange fronts. The more a beaver uses its teeth, the sharper they get for cutting.

The beaver's back molars are special too. They are as sharp and bumpy as a cheese grater. A beaver uses these teeth to grind up about 500 grams (more than a pound) of tree bark every day.

Special Food

You may prefer ice cream, but tree bark is a beaver's favorite food. When a beaver is eating, it looks just like someone enjoying a cob of corn. It holds and turns a branch between its paws as it nibbles away at the tasty bark. Beavers do most of their feeding inside their homes or in the water where they are safest from hungry animals.

One good thing about eating tree bark is that you can always have a snack before the hard work of cutting down a tree.

In the spring and summer, beavers like to eat juicy shrubs and tree buds. During the fall, they eat more bark than usual and put on extra fat for the winter. They cut down many trees and gnaw them into short pieces. These are stored in big underwater piles near their homes. When the ice freezes over the top of their pond, the beavers have enough food stored to last the winter.

It doesn't happen often, but some winters the pond may freeze all the way through. Unable to swim to their underwater food store, the beavers could die of hunger. But beavers are lucky. Their homes are built from the same thing they eat—branches! As long as the winter doesn't last too long, the beavers can survive by eating bits of their home.

A tender summer leaf is always good for a nibble.

Opposite page:
A beaver will usually work alone when cutting down a tree.

The Beaver At Work

If you have ever had the painful experience of biting your tongue, you know how strong your chewing muscles are. A beaver's chewing muscles are much stronger than yours. With these powerful muscles and its very sharp teeth, a single beaver may cut down more than 200 trees every year!

When cutting, a beaver stands on its hind legs and leans back against its broad tail. It cuts with its head held sideways. The grooves left by the beaver's sharp teeth run across the tree trunk in the same direction as the marks left by an axe.

Beavers are messy workers. Instead of chewing out neat slices, a beaver takes several bites from the top of a cut and several bites from the bottom. Then it yanks out the wood that is left in the middle. The beaver's top teeth do most of the cutting while the bottom teeth help to steady its mouth.

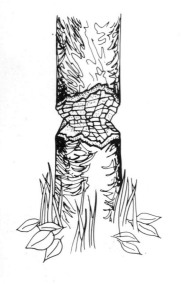

Grooves left by beaver's teeth.

Many people think that a beaver can make a tree fall whichever way it wants. It cannot, and it does not even know which way a tree it is cutting will fall. That is why a beaver cuts only until its teeth feel the last bits of wood just starting to break. Then—*swoosh!*—the beaver dashes for the safety of its pond.

The crash of the falling tree can be heard all over the forest. Before leaving the pond, the beaver waits and sniffs the air to make sure that no hungry bears or cougars have followed the sound in search of a beaver lunch.

Getting it Home

When all seems safe, the beaver and its family will begin cutting off the branches and dragging them back to their pond. If a log is too heavy for one beaver to carry in its mouth, two beavers will work together, rolling the log along the ground with their front paws.

It can seem like a long way to the pond when you have to drag a branch this size with you.

Once the trees near the pond are used up, beavers may have to move the logs quite a distance. Sometimes, when this happens, they dig canals that carry water from the pond closer to the trees. Then they can simply float the heavy logs back home. Beavers have been known to dig canals as much as 100 metres (328 feet) long.

Building the Dam

The perfect beaver pond is deep and surrounded by lots of trees. Beavers need to build their homes in deep ponds so that the underwater entrances are well covered. They also need deep water to keep the pond from freezing solid in the winter. To make their ponds deep enough, beavers build dams.

A dam works like the plug in your bathtub. The plug stops the tap water from running down the drain. Beavers build dams across the low banks or creeks where water could flow out of their ponds. With these exits sealed, the water from incoming streams gets trapped in the pond, making it very deep.

Nature's Engineers

Beavers are born knowing how to build dams. They start their building by holding large sticks in their mouths and driving them straight into the river bottom. Almost everything that a beaver can find goes into the dam—wood, grass, rocks and sometimes an old flashlight or shoe.

A beaver dam is built like a layer cake. Just as the cake is held together by layers of icing, the dam is held together by layers of mud. It is sometimes said that beavers use their tails to hammer in branches and spread mud when building dams, but this is not true. Beavers use

To keep the water where they want it, beavers must always be ready to patch up their dams.

28

their paws and noses to smear the mud over their dam.

Beavers will build until the sound of water running out of their pond has stopped. This sound is such an important signal for the beavers that scientists have been able to trick them into building dams by playing tape recordings of trickling water sounds.

Beaver Meadows

People get angry when a beaver's dam floods a road or field. It is true that beaver dams can sometimes be a nuisance, but they can be useful too—and not just to beavers! Beaver ponds become home to many new plants and animals. Grazing cattle often drink from them. And many years later, after the dam has rotted away and the pond has dried up, the soil will be very rich for farming. This land, which was once covered by a beaver pond, is known as a beaver meadow.

A Home of Sticks and Mud

When the dam is finished, the beavers start to work on a home. There is a lot of variety in beaver homes—in fact, no two are exactly alike.

If the beavers live in a pond that has very high banks they may simply dig a burrow in the side and live there. When the banks are low, beavers build a special kind of home—called a lodge—in their pond.

Building the Lodge

The beavers start their lodge by anchoring sticks in the bottom of the pond and piling a huge mound of branches on top. With every member of the family helping, the mound soon reaches high above the water. The branches are cemented together with thin mud. Carrying the mud in their paws or under their chins, the beavers dash as far up the slippery sides of the lodge as they can get. The mud that they dump flows down the sides, covering the lodge like syrup on a stack of pancakes.

Because the beavers seldom make it all the way up, the top gets very little mud. The mudless roof is important. It allows plenty of fresh air to get in the lodge.

Making it Comfortable
When the outside is almost finished, the beavers dive under water and begin to chew a tunnel through to the centre of the mound. They make a large living room above water level and then cut out at least one more entrance tunnel. The doorways to the tunnels are hidden underwater so that bears and wolves will not be able to get in.

Beavers will stay in the same pond and live in the same lodge as long as there are plenty of trees in the area. Like most homeowners, they spend a lot of time improving their lodges. As the family grows, additions are built to make the lodge roomy enough for everyone.

When there is work to be done, the whole beaver colony pitches in.

This is what you might see if you could slice off one side of a typical beaver lodge. While from the outside the lodge looks like a pile of sticks, inside it is a comfortable home.

During the winter, the beaver family stays warm by snuggling together inside their home. Even when the temperature outside drops to -50°C, (-58°F) the heat of the beavers' bodies keeps the inside of the lodge above the freezing point. A blanket of snow on the lodge helps trap heat inside too.

When a beaver gets hungry in the winter, it takes a deep breath and swims out the tunnel to the underwater food pile that was built in the fall.

The Beaver Family

Cows live in herds and chickens live in flocks. But beavers live in family groups just as you do. A beaver family is called a colony.

A mother and father beaver stay together for their whole lives. Though both parents help to raise the babies, it is the mother who makes the final decisions in a beaver colony.

Beavers mate each year in late January or early February. During the breeding season, the beaver pair spend a lot of time frolicking and play-wrestling below the icy covering of their pond. The beavers mate during some of these underwater play sessions.

A female beaver has to wait three and a half months for her babies to be born. While she is waiting, she prepares a special nursery inside the lodge. She builds warm, comfortable beds for her babies by splitting soft wood into thin chips.

A beaver mother likes to be alone when her babies are born. Shortly before they arrive, the father leaves the lodge and moves into a burrow on the edge of the pond. When the birth time comes, the mother beaver sits up with her tail between her legs and carefully licks each baby as it is born. Beavers usually have a litter of four babies, called kits.

Beaver kits are born with a tiny set of sharp front teeth, a thick furry coat, and a flat scaly tail.

Beaver Babies

Weighing a little more than a baseball, each wide-eyed kit looks like a tiny copy of its parents. It even has a tiny set of sharp front teeth.

Beaver kits never need to take swimming lessons. They can swim a few hours after they are born! Their thick fur coats trap so much air that the kits bob along the water surface like corks. In fact, the babies float so well that they cannot dive until they have gained a few pounds. But since a floating kit would be an easy catch for a hungry hawk or otter, the mother keeps her babies inside the lodge for the first two months.

Just like new human babies, beaver kits wake up every few hours and cry to be fed. They often sit on their mother's tail when they are nursing. Beaver milk is butter-yellow and as thick as toothpaste. This rich milk helps the babies grow quickly.

Beaver parents teach their kits to dive when they hear a tail slap against the water.

A Lot to Learn

The kits learn many things by copying their parents and older brothers and sisters. When they see an older beaver chewing on a leaf, they rush over to have a taste. If another beaver dives for a branch, they dive too.

One important lesson the kits must learn is how to recognize danger. They are taught to sniff the air for the smell of wolves, cougars and bears and to watch and listen for otters, hawks and owls.

Both beaver parents are quick to help a whining kit. They will often carry them from danger by holding them in their mouths or scooping them up in their arms.

Growing Up

Beaver youngsters live with their parents for two years. Since a new litter is born every year, this means that a typical beaver family has about ten members—mother and father, one-year-olds (called yearlings) and kits.

The yearlings usually move out with their father for two weeks or so when the new litter

is being born. By this time, they are helping with the cutting and carrying chores, and with any needed repairs to the dam or lodge.

At two years of age, the young beavers are ready to leave home. They have to leave to make room for a new litter of kits. Most of them go quite willingly, but once in a while a straggler needs to be sent off with a hiss or a slap.

The young beavers may travel far before they settle down. Most, however, will pick a spot within 10 kilometres (6 miles) of their parents' pond. They soon find mates and set to work busily building dams and lodges for their own new colonies.

Words to Know

Breeding season   The time of year during which animals will mate.

Burrow   A hole dug in the ground by an animal for use as a home.

Canal   A path that is dug out for water to follow.

Castoreum   Oily substance produced by glands in the beaver's body and used to mark its territory.

Colony   A group of the same kind of animals living together.

Dam   A kind of wall built to hold back water.

Guard hairs   Long coarse hairs that make up the outer layer of a beaver or other animal's coat.

Kit   Name for the young of various animals, including the beaver.

Litter   Young animals born together.

Lodge   Beaver home built in the water, out of logs, sticks and mud.

Mate   To come together to produce young.

Molars   Large back teeth used for grinding.

Nurse   To drink milk from a mother's body.

Rodent   Any of a group of animals with front teeth especially adapted for gnawing.

Territory   Area that an animal or group of animals lives in and often defends from other animals of the same kind.

Webbed feet   Feet in which the toes are joined together by flaps of skin.

Yearling   Animal that is one year old.

INDEX

beaver meadow, 31
building dams, 27, 28, 31

canal, 27
castoreum oil, 12
chewing muscles, 22
coat, 8, 11
cutting trees, 22, 23

danger, 12, 44
description, 8, 11, 12
diet, 18, 21

ears, 14

fall, 21
family, 35, 38-44
feet, 14, 17
flooding, 31

gophers, 7
grooming, 11
growing up, 44

hearing, 12
home, 21, 27, 32-38

kits, 38, 40, 43, 44

lodge, 32, 35, 38, 40
lungs, 14

mating, 40
movement, 8, 14, 17

nostrils, 14

predators, 24, 35, 43, 44

rats, 7
rodents, 7, 8

seeing, 12, 14
smelling, 12
spring, 21
squirrels, 7
summer, 21
swimming, 8, 11, 14, 43

tail, 8, 14, 22
teeth, 7, 17, 18, 22, 43

waterproof, 11, 12
where found, 7
winter, 21, 27, 38

yearlings, 44

Cover Photo: Valan Photos, Wayne Lankinen
Photo Credits: Network Stock Photo File: page 4 (Jacob Formsma); Valan Photos: 6, 42 (J.A. Wilkinson), 9, 45 (Wayne Lankinen), 13 (John Fowler), 16 (Harold V. Green), 19, 29 (Dennis W. Schmidt), 25 (Val & Alan Wilkinson), 26 (Brian Milne); Norman R. Lightfoot: 10, 15, 30, 33, 39, 41; Lowry Photography: 20, 23; NFB Phototèque: 34:

Printed and Bound in Spain